Christ
Before
Creation

Christ
Before
Creation

AN INTRODUCTION TO A TRANSCENDENT LORD

and to

THE CHRONICLES OF HEAVEN

Gene Edwards

SeedSowers Publishing
Jacksonville, Florida

Library of Congress Cataloging-in-Publication Data

Edwards, Gene
    Christ, Before Creation : The Chronicles of Heaven / Gene Edwards
    ISBN 0-940232-0-49
    1. Bible Fiction. I. Title.

SeedSowers Publishing
P.O. Box 3317
Jacksonville, FL 32206
800-228-2665
www.seedsowers.com

Dedication

To Paul and Judy Schiebe
Friends of the long haul

Books by Gene Edwards

The Chronicles of Heaven
Christ Before Creation
The Beginning
The Escape
The Birth
The Triumph
The Return

The First-Century Diaries
The Silas Diary
The Titus Diary
The Timothy Diary
The Priscilla Diary
The Gaius Diary

A Tale of Three Kings
The Prisoner in the Third Cell
Letters to a Devastated Christian
Exquisite Agony
Dear Lillian
The Day I was Crucified
One Hundred Days in the Secret Place

Introduction to the Deeper Christian Life
Living by the Highest Life
The Secret to the Christian Life
The Inward Journey

Radical Books for Radical Christians
Rethinking Elders
Climb the Highest Mountain
Revolution, The Story of the Early Church
How to Meet in Homes
Beyond Radical

In a Class by Itself
The Divine Romance

Introduction

In order to touch the depths of Jesus Christ, you must become familiar with *the other realm*, the realm of the invisible.

Christ Before Creation serves as a small step in introducing you to an understanding of the unseen realm. It is also a part of a series which will introduce you to *The Chronicles of Heaven*. Both awaken your spirit to awareness of that realm, the realm of *your* spirit. As you begin the journey into the realm of worlds unseen, always remember Paul's words:

> You have been given all the riches
> of heavenly places which are in
> Christ Jesus.   *Eph.1:3*

There are week-long retreats held in Roanoke, Alabama each year which serve to give you practical handles for an incredible walk with Christ. (It is also a week spent in silence.) This retreat is about "Learning to Fellowship with Jesus Christ outside Space and Time."

There are books that everyone is to read *before* arriving at the retreat grounds. Those books include *Christ Before Creation* and *The Chronicles of Heaven*.

Whether or not you attend this retreat, these books are here to awaken your spirit to the other realm, to a place without dimension, time or space: the place where Christ lives in you.

Welcome to the first glimpses of the realm where Christ dwells.

CHAPTER
One

We are going to take a trip back in time. From there we will go to a place *before* time.

It is, more accurately, a place that never existed. That is, it is not a place as we think of in terms of dimension.

Where we are going is not in this creation. Because this "place" is non-dimensional, it does not meet the qualifications of being *a place*. There is no time there, no space, no up, no down, and no measurement.

Where is this *non*-place?

The place is God Himself.

God, before creation.

God is without dimension; therefore, we cannot say that "in God" is a place.

As we move into God, we make a discovery. We see Christ at God's very center, and there we see Christ as He was before creation.

Christ *did* exist before creation.

What was Christ, the Creator, like *before* He created? And what did He *do* before He created? There are many things Christ did before creation. He was very active before He created.

1

To go *into God before creation* means we journey to a time before time—a place when there was no place, no space, no measurement, and no tick of the clock. These concepts were nonexistent. To journey to the point before creation means we leave *everything* behind. There are no angels. No heavenlies. No earth. No skies. Not even . . . *nothingness*!

Nothingness did not exist—no "vast void" at that time before time. There was no anything except *God*.

There were not two things: God and nothingness. There was God and only God. Not God plus nothingness. Not God plus anything. God was *all*!

Nonetheless, this *non*-dimensional place, which is God Himself, is the one and only place where we can safely say that all things that are there are *real*. This is a place where there are no shadows, no types, no replicas, no images, no pictures of that which is real.

In God, no unrealities. Yes, God is a place that is before symbols.

God . . . the only place where *all* is reality! This we *must* understand if we are to grasp Christ before creation.

CHAPTER
Two

We live in a world of shadows, symbols, types, images and pictures. For instance, we speak of gold; but the gold we have here in the material realm is made of mass, filled with protons, electrons and atoms, in a place that gives us no more than a picture of real gold. Real gold is Christ. Our gold, here in the realm of mass, is a suggestion of Christ. Also, the *real* sun is Christ. Our sun is a shadow of Christ. It is a picture of Him.

Before creation there existed in the Father, in the Son, and in the Holy Spirit the *real gold*, the *real water*, and *real food*. There in God resided real water, food, light and life; and they are not shadows, nor symbols, nor images, nor reflections.

Before creation, gold was Christ. Water was Christ. Light was Christ. The sun was Christ. The moon was Christ. Then, along came creation. And creation was strewn with pictures of Him. That moon up in the sky is not the true reality. That moon is a picture of Christ.

Life was Christ. True Life *is* Christ. All we have here in the physical creation is a shadow of Life. Christ is *Life*!

Before creation began, Christ was *everything*, and

5

everything was Christ.

You and I and all things around us are shadows, pictures, images, replicas, and reflections of Christ!

What was *not* in God before creation?

CHAPTER
Three

What things were not present before creation? No law, no legalism, no rules, regulations or observances. Such things did not and could not exist. Mark this: There was no bondage. There was no prayer. There was fellowship, though. Prayer did not come until after creation and until after the Fall. Before that, fellowship reigned.

Freedom ran free. Freedom was nothing less than Christ Himself. The only thing there was the Father, the Son, and the Spirit. Nothing existed except the Godhead. All was reality. The only reality that ever existed, existed *there*.

The Trinity moved in a realm of absolute freedom, which is a natural, innate part of God. The Godhead was having a wonderful time! But what were they doing? The Godhead was fellowshipping. The Father, Son and Spirit were fellowshipping with one another. That is what they were doing.

That simple fact, a corporate fellowshipping of the Trinity, just may be the key to everything.

They fellowshipped? Yes, the Father was the glory of the Son. The Son, the glory of the Father. The Father adored the Son; the Son adored the Father. The Holy Spirit was the transport.

So it was that one non-day, in the midst of this rich, unobstructed, immutable fellowship, the Godhead called a counsel. They counseled with one another and then agreed with their counsel.

The Godhead decided that eyes other than the eyes of God should see the glory of the Son. Such eyes which were not yet should see how glorious is the Son.

The Godhead colluded together and decided to do something that one might say was a terrible gamble. Having made this awesome decision (which included the gamble), they worked out a plan, a purpose, which guaranteed that the gamble would be no gamble at all.

What the Godhead decided was immutable, for the Godhead decided that there would be portions of the Son that would be chosen for some marvelous destiny. These portions of Christ were predestined, predetermined to a glorious destiny. Those portions of Christ were *marked out* for the incredible. In that non-time, it also strongly appeared that those blessed portions of Christ would one day be separated from Christ. But it only *seemed* that way.

A gamble that was no gamble, a separation that was no separation at all. His plan would resolve all these

paradoxes. Those portions, though seemingly separated after space and time arrived, had never been anywhere except *in Christ*. It simply is not possible to separate part of the Son from the Son. All of God is in every part of God!*
Be it the Father, or the Son, or the Spirit, all that is of the Father is in the Father. All that is *in all of the Son*, and all that is *in all of the Spirit* is in every part of God. A portion of God contains all of God.

So we have two enigmas: A gamble that is no gamble at all; and parts of the Son, appointed for some future destiny in space-time, remaining in the Son and containing all of the Son. Portions of Christ . . .

Chosen.

Predestined.

Predetermined.

Those portions of Christ awaited their purpose somewhere out there in the future appearance of the space-time continuum. But these glorious portions could only have their destiny fulfilled if a creation appeared. Then the great drama of those marked-off portions would begin.

Absolutely no one knew anything about all this activity. But that is because there *was* no one else. You might say that the marked off, predestined ones remained a *mystery*. A mystery hidden exactly where it should be. A mystery hid-

*John 3:34b

den in God. A mystery known only to God. Later, after creation came into existence, we in creation would hear whispers of all these things; but until a very special moment in time, all this activity remained only rumors.

So it is that we see, there was a great deal of activity before creation.

And just what else might there be?

CHAPTER
Four

What else happened before creation? For one thing, just before creation, something was present which was *not* God.

After the destined ones were chosen, and just before creation, there appeared a book. This book listed the names of all the "marked-off" ones. In this book the Lord wrote the names of all the *destined ones*.

Did this book have a name? Yes, the book was called *The Book of Life*. This is because it contained the names of all who would receive God's own Life in them. These are the very ones who would receive *eternal life*.

What is eternal life? Eternal life is a life form — God's own Life. That form of life, the highest of all life forms, is also called divine Life.

Christ — *He is* divine Life!

So it was that the Godhead wrote the names of those portions of Christ into the Book of Divine Life. In it was a record of all who would one day in time have divine Life. It was a record of those who would have Christ *in* them.

Out there in the distant future, it was also ordained that one day all those portions would come together. Or should we say *come together again*? In that coming together, they would once more be utterly one, just as they were all originally one—part of Christ and one with Christ.

In that future hour, when all those portions would come together, they would then become utterly one with one another and utterly one with Christ. Yet we must add, in this mysterious enigma, those marked-off portions of Christ were always, past and future, one with each other, and *always* in Christ.

Having written all those names in the Book of Divine Life, the Son closed the book and sealed it. He sealed the book with the understanding that nothing could change God's selection of those chosen ones. *All* would be there, as part of Him, at the very end and into the *forevermore*.

Once that book closed, *nothing* could prevent what God had purposed to accomplish. Those portions, those names, were *guaranteed* to forever *stay in Christ*. No event could change that.

So, before creation there was God as all, a choosing, and a Book.

As wonderful as all this is, these were not the only events that took place with Christ before creation.

There would be more, much more, that would happen.

CHAPTER
Five

Christ Before Creation

The Lord stepped forth onto the precipice upon which He would create. Would this be the moment when there would be *other than God*?

No, there was still more for Him to do before the actual act of creating. Several amazing things took place.

Have you ever seen a little lamb? A lamb is really but a picture that tells us what Christ is like. Christ is the real Lamb.

Remember that terrible gamble (which will turn out to be no gamble at all)? Once creation came into existence, God would allow all things to take their course, so things might *not* work out as God planned; hence, the gamble. But God did awesome things before creation to guarantee that all would work out as He planned, even though creation's inhabitants were free to plot their own destiny. And so it came to pass that before creation, all things were . . .well, it is a little hard to explain, so let us watch the drama.

Just before the act of creation, the Father *slew* His only Son. He slew the Lamb. The Father did this *before* creation. Never before had He slain His Son, nor would He ever again!

19

Christ *truly* died *before* creation, before space-time.

Christian, this is your Lord.

At the moment of the slaying of the Lamb, all those portions of Christ also died. What happened to Christ happened to them. His death was their death. Those marked-off portions of Christ were of Him, from Him, through Him, but most of all . . . *in* Him, when He died.

And also when He rose!

This dying and rising happened before time, before dimension, before space, *before* creation.

Once, and only once, these predestined portions of Christ died with Christ and in Christ, never again to die.

When He rose, all those portions were still part of Him and therefore rose with Him and in Him. They rose but once. Never before and never again.

Neither Christ nor the parts of Christ could ever die again. Death could not touch Him. Nor can Death ever again touch them!

So, you see, much did happen before creation.

All these marvelous *secret* things took place *before* He created. What an incredible Christ.

All this is Christ before creation!

Nonetheless, as glorious as is all this, we have yet to

come to the main point.

    Now we must face the inexplicable.

    Just before creation . . . .

CHAPTER
Six

Christ Before Creation

Certainly, you and I must say that we were in that creation and we are part of that creation . . . or so we think.

That you and I are in this creation and of this creation is not entirely correct. Of a truth we were *not* in this creation when it came into existence. As the pages of the history of this creation unfold, it strongly appears that you *are* of this creation; yet, as enigmatic as it is, you are *not* of the creation which Christ was just about to create.

No, you cannot be of this creation because you *precede* creation!

After all, you were in Christ . . . *before*. When He visited here, He had a habit of speaking about *before*.

For instance, He said:

"*Before* Abraham was, I AM!"

"Those whom You gave Me *before* . . . ."

And in that moment, when He made those startling statements, *you* were *in* Him. You were there before Abraham. Why? Because you are, and were, in Christ.

It is an oddity of this creation (the one Christ was about to create) that it has a clear, distinct beginning and an absolute end. Every atom, every molecule will be gone.

You will be present at that end. All things vanish. All! So, will *you* also vanish? If you vanish, then you truly are part of this creation. But if you do not vanish, then we can say you are *not* part of this creation. In the eyes of God, *you* are not involved in, or part of, this creation. Citizenship of this creation does not include you.

Let us return to that moment just before Christ was about to call into existence creation.

You were chosen in Christ and were part of Christ *before* He called creation into existence. (Part of you may be a great deal older than you realize. A part of you has been around a very long time. Even before time!)

That is not all . . . there was the choosing, the slaying of that Lamb, the creation of man, the fall of man, the fall of creation, the cross in Jerusalem, Christ's death, His resurrection, your redemption and, finally, the dissolving of this fallen creation. In mysteries beyond mysteries, all this was done away with *before* He created anything. To put it another way, Christ did away with creation *before* He created creation!

How is it possible for Him to destroy something He had not created? It is inexplicably true! Christ can do this. He does, you know! Your Lord finished all things before He created all things.*

*Heb. 4:3

How? The answer has to do with Christ's dwelling outside the passing of time.

Remember that your Lord was doing all these acts in a realm where there is no space, no time, no up, no down, no mass, no measurement . . . no past, no present, no future. All that He did, He did in realms unseen, in that non-place called the *eternal now*! When space and time came into existence, the events that took place in the *eternal now* intersected with space-time. It is possible for the eternals to invade time and establish, in time, events that took place in the eternals. The events, thereby, happened in a realm of time, the seen realm. Suddenly, what had happened in eternity was becoming real in time.

These events occurred before mass, before creation . . . before anything! That is, anything except God. And God made sure He had finished everything before He created *anything*!

Dare we explore this enigma further?

CHAPTER
Seven

Creating creation, giving man free will, and risking the Fall really did appear to be a staggering gamble on the Lord's part, but it was not so. Christ meant to accomplish everything first in eternity, to see that His will was carried out before He created.

Redemption was there before the Fall, before creation. Therefore, what appeared, in our eyes, to be a vast gamble had been taken care of before He said "Let there be . . . ."

There were things done before creation that took care of crises that would happen *after* creation. When space-time did come along, the timeless intersected with time; the unlocatable intersected with the locatable. The realities of what had happened *before* gradually became revealed *during* time.

This is all inexplicable, of course. Things occurred on planes beyond our understanding.

We really need to know only one thing: In realms of timelessness, your Lord resolved all the crises that would later occur in creation.

To illustrate, you have seen that when your Lord was slain by His Father, those who were in Him died with Him, too. When Christ was slain, He took not only you, but also the creation (which had not yet been created), into death. Furthermore, the Fall (which had not yet occurred), and a Cross (which had not come), and a Satan (who did not yet exist), and Death (which had never been known), as well as the heavens and the earth (which were not yet created) . . . all were taken into His being, and they all died with Him. He died! He went into a grave (a grave that was *not yet*). There, in the grave, He destroyed all those things.

Christ slew you, fallen man, the fall itself, the sin of the world, death, the principalities, the powers, the law, and the entire world system when He was slain, before the foundations of the world. All of it was annihilated in that instant just before creation. Before creation, before *all else,* the Lamb took care of everything. The Lamb destroyed that which was not yet. A creation that had not been was placed in Him and then put to death . . . before He created it.

Know this: The world you presently live in has imprinted on the back of its neck these words:

CRUCIFIED BEFORE CREATED

No wonder Christ is so assured about the final outcome: This creation was destroyed on the Cross before it was created.

Before creation, not only was Christ slain by His

Father, but so was everything else.

But what of the resurrection?! This, too, took place before creation came into being.

Resurrection, before? Yes! This is why Christ could declare, "I am resurrection."

Resurrection is Christ. Christ rose before anything was created . . . out there in a spaceless, timeless, unseen, unknown, incomprehensible realm.

What of all the things that were not Christ which also died in Him? They were not of Him, nor were they He Himself! Did they rise? No. In His pre-creation death, all other things were destroyed. They ceased to exist. The creation and all things in creation ceased to exist . . . forever. And, it happened *before*!

You must understand that this creation has *already* been slain and done away with.

Amazing is it not? Incomprehensible is it not? We stand in awe of this incomparable Christ who is before creation.

And part of you existed in that incomparable Christ before creation.

Still, we have not come to the main point.

Now we come to yet greater revelation of this Christ who was before creation.

33

We are about to see the greatest release of power that Christ ever unleashed.

We now come to that moment when the triumphant resurrected Lord created.

That begs a question. If in that primordial age the Lord was all, then where did He place creation? There was no "out there" because Christ was *all*.

Where, then, did Christ place creation? He could not place creation *beside* Him. There was no "beside" Him. After all, there was no place for even *nothingness*! There was no way to create creation *without*. Creation had to be created *in Christ*! (He is that great!) Creation, inside Him: That is where this creation is located, even today. Creation is *inside Christ your Lord*.

If you can *see* that creation in Christ, you can also see the resolution of much of the paradoxes, mysteries, and enigmas of our faith. After all, words like predestined, chosen, preordained, and foreknown could very easily raise a number of questions, especially when you add the words *free will*. If we see the greatness of Christ before creation, the paradoxes vanish.

This creation has a physical, geographic location; that is, creation is geographically locatable. Creation is located *in Christ*.

Today, right now, where is creation? In Christ. Christ envelops creation.

Such is the greatness of your Lord!

Now we move a little further into this greatest of mind-boggling mysteries. Both *the beginning* and *the end* of creation are *in* Christ. There is a vast history in between these two statements: "In the beginning . . . " (Genesis 1:1); and "the first heaven and the first earth passed away" (Revelation 21:1). One statement tells us about the beginning of creation, the other about the end of creation. Remember, if creation is in Christ, then Christ is at the beginning and the end simultaneously.

The dawn of creation starts at the beginning. On and on the story unfolds. He who is Alpha *and* Omega watches the drama. The drama reveals to us Enoch, Noah, Abraham, Moses, and David. Then the Cross and the tomb appear. Then there is Peter and there is Paul. As the drama continues to move forward, someone who looks a lot like *you* appears.

All this drama is *in Him*.

Christ *was* at the beginning of this drama, and Christ *is* at the end of this drama. Understand how this is possible. Christ envelops creation on all sides, making both ends of the drama happen at the same time because both are in Him.

Over here is the beginning; over there, the end. Where is Christ? Is Christ stuck at the beginning? Is He stuck *here,* today? Is He stuck at *the end?*

If He is stuck *here*, now, that would mean He would not know who made it to the end. That would rob Him of being the Omega, the end.

But Christ is stuck nowhere. He is in all places at all times because all places and all time are in Him. We might say that Christ need not even move, because time is moving inside Him. Space-time began at the beginning and moves forward in Him. When space-time comes to the end of its existence, that final, last moment is also in Him. He is there at the beginning; He is at the end. All is in Him.

This means the front and the back, the top and the bottom, the beginning and the end are in Christ. We cannot say of Christ that He is the Alpha and someday out there in the future He will become the Omega. Right now Christ is at the beginning and at the end of time, at the beginning and end of this creation. Both, right now. There is where He *is*. There is where He always is. Right now your Lord is at the end. He not only sees the end, He *is at* the end. Right now He is also at the beginning. There is where He is and where He always is.

Can we understand this? Of course not. We are shackled to three dimensions and captured in a seventy-year time frame . . . in time, in space . . . *here*.

Outside space and time, Christ at the beginning and the end simultaneously, was not something that John Calvin understood. He was caught in space-time, too. Calvin had a God who was trapped in *the present*. Armenius had the same problem.

One of those men said "eternal security"; that is, once saved always saved! The other man said, "free will"; that is, you can lose your salvation. Armenius said your name could be taken out of the Book of Life; Calvin said, "No it cannot."

Neither man grasped a revelation of Christ before creation, nor did they understand that creation is in Christ.

Is there a way out of this dilemma?

Can there be reconciliation? Yes, as we shall see.

CHAPTER
Eight

See a Lord, free of space-time, who is at the beginning when the names of the redeemed are placed in the Book of Life. Christ is also at the end, and at the end there is the great throng of the redeemed, the gathering of all the redeemed in one place. We *know* for sure that these saints described in Revelation 7 "made it"! They are all saved. On this point Calvin and Armenius agree! But Calvin would explain: "These were chosen before creation; none fell away. They are *all* here at the end, but were chosen at the beginning; and nothing can change that."

Armenius, looking at the same throng, would declare: "Oh, no, God chose many more than these; but they exercised their free will, rejected the Lord, and/or some fell into grievous sin. Those who did not make it had their names taken out of the Book of Life."

It therefore came to pass that two separate views, one called Calvinism, the other Armenianism, arose! Neither fully grasped "in." But we need not look down on these two men; we do not understand "in" either.

There need be no difficulty here. As we pass through time, from the creation to the end, man can, and does, exercise free will. He does so all throughout his journey. Total *free will*. God does not interfere. However, a sovereign Christ preordained us, created creation, destroyed creation, and knows the names of everyone in that great throng of the redeemed. He did the choosing and the predestining at the beginning.

Predestination *and* free will? How so? Is that not impossible?

Not if you see that creation is *in* Christ and that Christ is at the beginning . . . where He always is, and Christ is at the end . . . where He always is.

May I now present to you the free will of man and the security of the believer, reconciled.

Be advised, however, this was not written to discuss Calvinism and Armenianism. This is to reveal to you the greatness of Christ before creation and the greatness of Christ with creation in Him.

See free will and then see the result of that free will, at the *end*. The redeemed were chosen at the beginning, based on the fact that they had already been seen at the end.

In that glorious moment at the end—where Christ always is—your Lord sees the redeemed ones and He moves backward through time until He comes to the *beginning* . . . where He always is. There He writes the names of the redeemed in the Book of Life based on those who made it to the end, based on the names of those who are in the great throng of the redeemed. Can He do that? Yes, because He is at the beginning and at the end . . . where He always is.

Let us see all this through the eyes of Christ. Christ says, "I know they made it and will be there at the end because I am at the end—where I always am—and I saw them there, so I place those names in the Book of Life. I did so before the beginning, where I am, where I always am."

There, before the beginning, where Christ is, where He always is, He opens the Book of Life. He writes in the names of all those redeemed ones who were at the end. You know, those people whom Calvin and Armenius both agree are "the ones who made it."

This should make both Calvinists and Armenians happy!

Are you wondering how it will all turn out at the end? Who will be saved to the very end?

Will *you* make it there to the very end?

Let us do what Christ did. He went to the end, where He is, where He always is; and while He was moving from the beginning to the end, He passed all places and all times, where He is, where He always is. He passed through the space-time continuum in all places, for He is there, no matter where "there" is. *

Christ also came to you in your time . . . where He is, where He always is. He said, "Look! One of the ones who is in Me, who was in Me at the beginning and was in Me before the beginning . . . where I am, where I always am." So Christ went back to the beginning, where He is, where He always is, and He opened the Book of Life to see if your name was written there. Lo and behold, there was your name — where it *always* is. Your name was in the Book of Life because you were at the end . . . where you are, where you always are.

Christ looked inside Himself and saw you, *in* Him . . . where you are, where you always are.

Then Christ did a double check on you. He came at last to the very end, where He is, where He always is; and, lo and behold, He saw you yet again. He saw you there in the great throng of the redeemed, singing "Thou art worthy, Thou art worthy."

He is always there. And you are always in Him. Why are you there? Because you are in Him before, at the beginning, and at the end. No matter where you are, you are always . . . *in Him*!

Having seen you in the great gathering of the redeemed, was He surprised? Did He call out, "Oh, you made it! You

* "*There*" is where He is, where He always is.

made it to the end. Oh that is wonderful!" Not likely! Perhaps this is what He did: Perhaps He said, "I am now going to choose, select, and predestine you. I will return to that time before time, before creation, before all things, where I always am, and there I will decide that you will be saved."

(He can do that, you know.)

Then He went to the place where you were when you were calling on Him. That was easy! After all, he found you at the end, and He saw your name in the Book of Life *before* the beginning. At that "non-time" He elected you, chose you, justified you, sanctified you *and* glorified you.

See your dimensionless Lord, with creation in Him!

And yet, as glorious as all this is, there is a point more glorious still that is yet to be seen.

CHAPTER
Nine

You definitely are one of those who "made it" to the end. But can we be certain of that? Let's put space-time in reverse, and see. Is it possible that we could say you were predestined at the end?

Perhaps your name was placed in the Book of Life at the *end*, and then the Book of Life was taken to "before the beginning!"

It does not matter where, when, or how! It is only that He did it. We will never fully understand the "how" until we escape the tyranny of space-time.

No matter where He is—at the beginning, middle or end—He is where He always is . . . and you are also there; you are always there.

Some Lord, is He not!

Again, I must say to you, this is not the main point.

In the meantime, do you have a low view of yourself? Then look at you, there in Christ before creation and there in that throng. In both places, you are so beautiful, pure and holy. You glow! In fact, because you were part of Christ in the beginning, and in Him you made it to the end, you are forever pure, honored, holy and indescribably flawless. Perfect and beautiful!

That is what you *always* are because you always *are* in Christ.

Further, you are *all* of that in both directions ← → in eternity past, in the present, and in eternity future!

There are some things you have a right to; there are some things you have no right to. You have no right to a basement-eye view of yourself. Somewhere out there in the mysteries of the eternals, where space and time just do not count, you are of the purest holiness. You share the holiness of God. Even today, you cannot be indicted. On this very day, you are blameless. No blame, no indictment, and absolutely no condemnation. You could be quite concerned about this as long as your thoughts are chained to this earth; but not in a realm where the clock does not tick, where past and future do not exist. Where you, being chosen in Christ before the foundation of the earth, and you, standing in the great throng of the redeemed, have both become one, you are as beautiful as the glorified Christ . . . because you are of Him and lost within Him.*

Down here on earth, none of us look very impressive. But out there where the end is already over with, the sons and daughters of God, of whom you are one, look glorious! If you could take flight from this fallen creation, if you

*Corinthians 14:25

could take flight from all space and time, and see what you already are—and what you have always been and what you will always be—you would be very impressed.

The Christ who is before creation, is He not becoming more glorious to you? Is He not ineffable, immutable in His glory? What a Christ we have!

But again, this is not my main point.

Ever more glorious things await us.

CHAPTER
Ten

Christ, somewhere in the eternals, cried out as did Adam, later in space-time, "I am alone! I have no counterpart!"

In that moment we see revealed Christ's purpose— His purpose for creating, His *eternal* purpose!

His purpose in creating is to become one with His *chosen Bride*. His chosen, His predestined Bride.

What is her content? She is made up of all those marked-off portions of Christ, predestined to some great, glorious purpose. When those parts of Christ come together at the end, there is a moment when there emerges out of that throng Christ's own Bride! Bone of His bone, spirit of His Spirit.

There, out *beyond* the end, Christ becomes one with her. She is, in that moment of utter oneness, spirit of His Spirit. Life of His Life. At last, out there beyond all time, there is finally, fully revealed *the mystery*.

Then the final scene, the scene of all scenes, the moment of all moments. Paul speaks of it in that mysterious passage in I Corinthians 14:25. In that moment of union, Christ and His Bride will dissolve into the Father. Then He, who was once the All, becomes the All in All.

Oneness with God, the final, ultimate state. The purpose beyond all other purposes.

Wonderful, is He not!

All this is who your Lord is. Christ before creation, Christ beyond creation.

Dare to behold this matchless Christ before, during, outside of, at the end and beyond the end. This is your awesome glorious Lord.

Back when the Godhead counseled together, the Godhead decided that Christ would have a beautiful Bride. A Bride to match Christ. Can we possibly fathom how beautiful *that* girl must be? A woman as glorious as the Christ of the cosmos.*

He is in her. She is in him. He is in the Father. The Father is in Christ. Ultimately, they all become indistinguishable. Christ, one with His chosen ones. One with you. One with us all. We are as much one with Christ as the Father is One with Christ!* *

You are part of not only where He is, but you are part of what He is. Part of you is His very content.

You belong, and always have belonged, *where He is.*

But still, that is not the point!

_____

*I Corinthians 1:15-20

**John 17

CHAPTER
Eleven

The old creation, gone.

Christ and His Bride, one.

The situation beyond the end of creation is quite similar to the way things were before creation, when He was the All. Out there He is not the all; He is the All in All.

Those portions of Christ who were at the beginning are also beyond the end. They are together, both *before* and *after*. Nor is it to be forgotten that they are in oneness in the middle, also.

Always one.

Before creation, dear honored one, *you* were in Him. Then time came along. You were still in Him. While He was dying as the Lamb (Revelation 13:8), you were in Him. When the Fall took place, *you* were in Him. When He rose from the dead in Jerusalem, you were in Him. You have been in Him ever since.

Out there, somewhere, when Christ allows this creation to dissolve (yet it has, of course, already dissolved), you will still be in Him. And remember, there will be no second creation to replace the old creation, but there will be *the new creation* revealed. The new creation is not made up of things created. The new creation is all that is left after the old creation disappears. This new creation is made up of things that are uncreated.

Christ, and you, precede and survive the dissolution of fallen creation.

Today you belong to *the new creation*. After the end, you will still be part of the new creation, which is made up of things uncreated. Also, behold, this new creation is *older* than the *old* creation. The new creation *preceded* the old creation and continues *after* the old creation!

Is that possible?

Jesus Christ is before creation and after creation. Furthermore, Christ and all the parts of Christ are the content of the new creation.

You *are* the content of that new creation! Even that is not quite enough. More specifically, that part of you which was *before* is not created. That is, the best part of you is not a creation. Your body is a thing created. It ends when the old creation ends and is then completely replaced by a translated body. Your soul is everlasting, but not eternal. Your soul has a beginning, but no end ($\rightarrow$ everlasting).

What of your spirit ($\leftarrow \rightarrow$ eternal)!

As we have seen, your spirit is not of the physical realm. Your spirit is from the other realm. It appears that the believer's spirit is not even *in* this realm or of this realm. Your spirit belongs to the invisible realm. That means two-thirds of you is in this realm, and one-third of you is in the invisible realm!

Let us look at that "one-third" part of you!

Christ has placed Himself in you, in that one-third of you. Your spirit and His Spirit have become one . . . indistinguishably *one*. Not a blend, but *one*.

Part of your spirit has Christ in it. The two are one (I Corinthian 6:17). Because Christ is not created, there is an aspect of you that is also not of this creation. This "part" of you is life. It is referred to as Eternal Life. That life is Christ!

When you believed on Christ, two things happened to you. First, your spirit was raised from the dead. Second, Christ made His Spirit one with your spirit. So, at the very least, a portion of you belongs with the eternals.

After the end of all things, Christ will be so much a part of your spirit that your spirit and His spirit will be indistinguishably one. You will have a translated body, a body permeated by Christ. You will have a soul transformed and permeated by Christ.

That is you, *beyond* the end. That will also be the state of *all* believers.

So it will be that Christ will have become all that is in all.

You have caught a glimpse of how great and glorious is Christ before creation. Now you have a glimpse of how glorious is Christ after creation ends.

But up until now everything that has been said is but a background to introduce you to *the main* point.

Let us discover . . . *the point*!

CHAPTER
Twelve

Your name is written in a book that records the names of those who have His content.

Is this not an incredible Christ? A Christ far beyond all we ever dreamed?

But that is not the point . . .

There is a point greater than all that has been said until now.

Let us see again just what Christ did before creation. In so doing, see your glorious Lord. Glorious things done by a glorious Lord. Consider the greatness of this Christ. The Christ *before.* Never forget, the Christ of the thirty-three years is also the Christ of the cosmos, the eternal Christ. The Christ who created such a vast physical universe that man has yet to find its end. This is your Lord!

It is the Father's desire that you know *this* Christ.

He destroyed and then He created. He created and then He destroyed.

This Christ, the Christ *before,* is the Christ the Father determined would be first in all things. This Christ is now the enthroned Christ. It is by the might and power of this Christ that all creation is held together. This Christ will also one day wipe creation all away. This Christ, who now lives beyond death, cannot die.

This Christ chose you before the foundation of the world. This Christ loved you before the foundation of the world. This Christ died for you before the foundation of the world. This Christ makes love to you every day. This Christ will bring all the portions of Himself together. Out of us will this Christ call forth His Bride. This Christ is going to marry that beautiful girl!

What a glorious Lord!

Today this Christ is the very content of the church. The ekklesia is the enlargement of this Christ. This Christ loves her, passionately, of whom you are a part.

This Christ is the first. This Christ sits enthroned. This Christ was and is . . . the *real* Lamb. This Christ is reality —the reality of all the shadows, types, symbols, images and pictures found so abundantly in creation. All creation is but a picture of this Christ.

Yet all that has been said of Christ pales in the glory of the main point. The *main* point is incomprehensible. It is this final, supreme fact which drove men like Paul!

This glorious Lord who created all things, this glorious Lord with all creation in Him, this Lord who finished all things before He created all things, this Lord who chose you in Himself before the foundation of the world, this Lord who wrote your name in the Book of Life, either before the beginning or at the end or somewhere in between, and who turned the greatest of all gambles into no gamble at all, this Christ who was slain before creation, this Christ who is the glory of the Father, this Christ who is the ALL, who will be, and is, the All who is in All, this Christ who is the beginning and end, this Christ who is free of, above and beyond and outside of, all space, time, and even eternity . . . this Christ has a point to make, a message to bring to you.

The point, the *main* point, the incomparable point, the point above all points, a point you must spend the rest of your life considering and laying hold of is:

This Christ **Lives in You!!!**

It was God's will to make known what are the riches of the glory of the mystery, and to make known to you that this Christ—the Christ before creation, the Christ beyond creation—*this Christ,* dwells in you!!

Christ *in you*: the Mystery! This awesome, endless, immense Christ is living in you right now.

He lives in you!

Upon what is the church built? The church is built on a revelation of *this* Lord, *this* Christ.

The
ultimate end
of this
revelation of Christ
is that
this Christ
lives
in
you !

...rejoice that your names are recorded in the other realm.

You shall see the Son of Man ascending into the other realm.

John 6:42

Your father Abraham rejoiced to see My Day, and he saw it and was glad.

John 8:56

I say to you, before Abraham was born, I am.

John 8:58

To the brothers and sisters in the church in Corinth. Do not look at the things you can see all around you, but rather look at the things that can't be seen. The things you see around you are here for a very short time, but the things that you can't see are eternal.

II Corinthians 4:18

You have the hope that is laid up for you in other realms.

Colossians 1:5

Christ is the image of the invisible God. All created things were created by Him, both things in the other realm and also on the earth. He created things visible and things invisible. Christ created all things and all things were created for Christ.

Colossians 1:15-16

Christ is before all creation. All creation holds together in Christ.

Colossians 1:17

There is a mystery which has been hidden to all generations but has now been revealed to God's holy ones... the mystery which is Christ in you.

Colossians 1:26

The Father has blessed me with every spiritual blessing that is in the other realm in Christ.

Ephesians 1:3

For our citizenship is in the other realm, and there in that realm, we eagerly await for a Savior, the Lord Jesus Christ, who will give us a new body, like His, so that we can live with Him in the other realm.

Philippians 3:20-21

God promised eternal life to us in the age which preceded all ages.

Titus 1:2

Creation was made by the speaking of God. The creation that we see is not made out of things visible but by the word of God.

Hebrews 1:3

Previously there have been no books written to show you how to lay hold of the invisible realm. The unseen realm, after all, is a place where there is no dimension, no space, nor time . . . one that cannot be measured.

There is no up or down or boundaries . . . . To say the least, then, this is hard to grasp. Few books or authors have therefore dared to speak of these matters. Nonetheless, it is also the realm of the spirituals, the natural habitat of your Lord. For this reason this realm bears much exploration.

Why not? Part of that realm is in you. The Lord has given you His Spirit. He did that at the time of your salvation. And never forget that your spirit is from that realm; it is free of space and time. Your spirit, which dwells in you, belongs to the unseen realm.

Your Lord abides in a realm where all things are the *eternal now*. So also does your spirit.

Moreover, it is in *this realm* that you touch the Lord!

The New Testament often makes reference to that realm, but those references are mostly overlooked. This is because we have a very objective view of our faith. Consequently, we are very unfamiliar with that realm.

It is the purpose of this book, *Christ Before Creation,* and also *The Chronicles of Heaven* (that is: *The Beginning, The Escape, The Birth, The Triumph,* and *The Return*) to give you unique insight into and a deep awareness of the realm of the invisibles.

That series was written to prepare you for a deeper walk with Jesus Christ.

Enjoy *The Chronicles of Heaven*, not only for their awesome beauty, but also because, ageless in nature, they are among the most powerful and dramatic pieces of Christian literature you will ever read !

And, as you see the Christian faith as viewed from the other realm, may you begin to become aware that two realms join; and the joining of your Lord and your spirit is the doorway between those two realms.

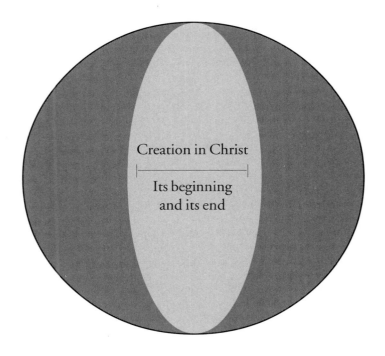

Creation in Christ

Its beginning
and its end

This circle represents the eternal and endless Christ.
The circle is open so you may see two things.
(1) You, deep inside Christ.
(2) The finite physical creation.
Creation is *in* Christ, but it is limited in existence, it has a
beginning and an end. You, on the other hand,
are always in Christ.

An Audio Tape Available

Before the release of this book, Gene Edwards brought a message, at Simpsonwood Christian Conference Center in Atlanta, Georgia, which is now entitled *Christ Before Creation*.

The message he delivered that day was recorded. When listening to it, you can hear, and even feel, the audience's astonished response. The message was, and is, electric. You may receive a free copy of this recording by writing:

SeedSowers
P.O. Box 3317
Jacksonville, FL 32206
1-800-228-2665
books@seedsowers.com

The Chronicles of Heaven
by
Gene Edwards

The Old Testament

The Beginning covers *Genesis*, chapters 1&2 (*The Promise* will come next, covering the rest of *Genesis*). *The Escape*, already in print, covers *Exodus*. Other volumes will follow until the Pentateuch is finished.

In *The Beginning* God creates the heavens and the earth. The crowning glory of creation, man and woman, live and move in both the visible world and the spiritual world.

Experience one of the greatest events of human history: *The Escape* of the Israelite people from Egypt. Watch the drama from the view of earthly participants and the view of angels in the heavens.

Experience the wonderful story of the incarnation of Jesus, seen from both realms. *The Birth* introduces the mystery of the Christian life for those who have never heard the story.

The New Testament

The Chronicles then extend into the New Testament. They are *The Birth* and *The Triumph*. After *The Triumph* comes *The First-Century Diaries*!

In *The Triumph* you will experience the Easter story as you never have before. Join angels as they comprehend the suffering and death of Jesus and the mystery of free will in light of God's Eternal Purpose.

The Door has moved to a hill on Patmos. What would John be allowed to see? *The Return* invites you to witness the finale of the stirring conclusion to *The Chronicles of Heaven*.

AN INTRODUCTION TO
THE DEEPER CHRISTIAN LIFE

In Three Volumes
by
Gene Edwards

Living by the Highest Life

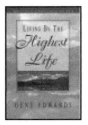

If you find yourself unsettled with Christianity as usual . . . if you find yourself longing for a deeper experience of the Christian life . . . *The Highest Life* is for you.

Did Jesus Christ live the Christian life merely by human effort? Or did Jesus understand living by the Spirit—His Father's Life in Him?

Discover what it means to live a spiritual life while living on earth.

I.

The Secret to the Christian Life

Read the Bible, pray, go to church, tithe . . . is this what it means to live the Christian life? Is there more to living the Christian life than following a set of rules? How did Jesus live by the Spirit?

The Secret to the Christian Life reveals the one central secret to living out the Christian life. Nor does the book stop there . . . it also gives *practical* ways to enhance your fellowship with the Lord.

II.

The Inward Journey

The Inward Journey is the companion volume to *The Secret to the Christian Life*. A beautiful story of a dying uncle explaining to his nephew, a new Christian, the ways and mysteries of the cross and of suffering. Of those who have a favorite Gene Edwards book, tens of thousands have selected *The Inward Journey* as that book.

III.

The Divine Romance

by
Gene Edwards

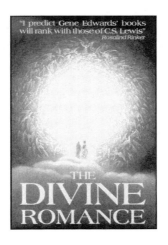

The Divine Romance is praised as one of the all-time literary achievements of the Protestant era. Breathtakingly beautiful, here is the odyssey of Christ's quest for His bride. *The Divine Romance* is the most captivating, heartwarming and inspirational romance, transcending space and time. In all of Christian literature there has never been a description of the crucifixion and resurrection which so rivals as the one depicted in *The Divine Romance*.

Many readers have commented, "This book should come with a box of Kleenex." The description of the romance between Adam and Eve alone is one of the great love stories of all times.

Edwards' portrayal of the romance of Christ and His bride takes its place along side such classics as Dante's *The Divine Comedy* and Milton's *Paradise Lost*. Reading this literary masterpiece will alter your life forever.

One of the greatest Christian classics of all time.

The First-Century Diaries

by

Gene Edwards

IF YOU NEVER READ ANY OTHER BOOKS ON THE NEW TESTAMENT
. . . READ *THE FIRST-CENTURY DIARIES*!

Here is more than what you would learn
in seminary! The Diaries will revolutionize your
understanding of the New Testament, and, in turn will revolutionize
your life. The best part is, this set of diaries reads like a novel. Never
has learning the New Testament been so much fun.

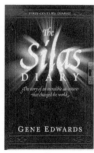

I.

The Silas Diary

This historical narrative parallels the book of Acts,
giving a first-person account of Paul's first journey.

The Silas Diary is your invitation to join Silas, Paul,
and their companions on a journey fraught with danger and
adventure - a journey that changed the history of the world.
Learn with the first-century Christians what freedom in
Christ really means.

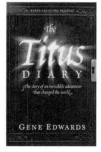

II.

The Titus Diary

This compelling narrative continues the events of the
Book of Acts. *The Titus Diary* is a firsthand account of
Paul's second journey as told by Titus.

Join this journey as Paul sets out once more-this time
with Silas, Timothy, and Luke-and learn of the founding of
the churches in Philippi, Thessalonica, Corinth, and Ephesus.
Look on as Paul meets Aquila and Priscilla and quickly gains
an appreciation of their passion for the Lord and His church.

The First-Century Diaries

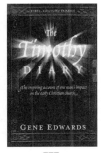

III.

The Timothy Diary

In *The Timothy Diary* Paul's young Christian companion Timothy gives a firsthand account of Paul's third journey.

This journey is quite different from Paul's others. It is the fulfillment of Paul's dream, for in Ephesus Paul trains a handful of young men to take his place after his death. Paul follows Christ's example in choosing and training disciples to spread the gospel and encourage the growth of the church.

IV.

The Priscilla Diary

Here are the stories of Paul's continued travels to the first-century churches narrated from the unique perspective of Priscilla, a vibrant first-century Christian woman!

See Paul writing his most personally revealing letter, his letter to the church in Corinth. Marvel at the truths Paul conveys to the church in Rome, a letter "of all that Paul considered central to the Christian life."

V.

The Gaius Diary

Paul and Nero meet face to face in a moment of highest drama.

Paul is released, but soon is arrested again, and again faces Nero. The sentence is death. Just before his execution, all the men he trained arrived in Rome to be with him. *The Gaius Diary* gives life-changing insight into Paul's final letters. Colossians, Ephesians, Philemon, and Philippians come alive as you see in living color the background to these letters. Be there in April of 70 A.D. when Jerusalem is destroyed.

For the first time ever in all church history, here is the entire first-century story from beginning to end.

THE NEW TESTAMENT
IN FIRST PERSON

The Story of My Life
as Told by Jesus Christ

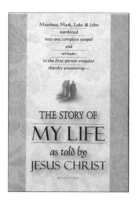

Listen to Jesus, the Christ, tell His own story. . . in His own words. . . to you !

All four Gospels have been combined in one single, flowing narrative. And it is in the first person! *The Story of My Life as Told by Jesus Christ* is a complete and thorough account of the events of Christ's life. Now you can read all of the Lord's life in chronological order, without repetition of a single detail. Every sentence in the Gospels is included, plus times, dates and places.

Allow yourself to be immersed into the setting of the life and ministry of Christ. Follow His footsteps as He walked the earth with those He knew and loved, in one smooth, flowing, uninterrupted story.

The impact is so arresting you will feel that you are hearing the gospel story for the first time. And always, in first person, the Lord is speaking directly to you. Think of it as *The Jesus Diary*.

Acts in First Person

For the first time in history, you can read the Acts of the Apostles in first person . . . like a diary.

Listen to the men who lived during the exciting early years of the church. Experience the excitement and danger as these men travel to declare Jesus Christ. Every detail is included . . . such as dates and location.

Based on Tyndale's New Living Translation Bible, *Acts in First Person* is in readable, contemporary English. A wonderful study aid for all ages.

Books that Heal

Hundreds of thousands of Christians all over the world have received healing while reading these books.

Exquisite Agony
(formerly titled *Crucified by Christians*)

Gene Edwards

Here is healing for hurting and disillusioned Christians who have known the pain of betrayal at the hand of another believer.

This book has brought restoration to Christians all over the world who had lost all hope. Edwards takes you to a high place to see your pain and suffering from the viewpoint of the Lord.

Read this book and learn the *privilege of betrayal* and discover who the real author of your crucifixion is!

Letters to a Devastated Christian

Gene Edwards

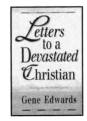

The Christian landscape is covered with the remains of lives ruined at the hands of authoritarian movements. Some believers never recover. Others are the walking wounded.

In *Letters to a Devastated Christian,* Edwards has written a series of letters to a brokenhearted Christian and points him to healing in Christ. This book is full of profound healing and hope.

The Prisoner in the Third Cell
Gene Edwards

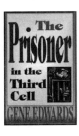

This is a book of comfort, told as an unforgettable drama, for those caught up in circumstances of life they do not understand.

In this dramatic story, John the Baptist, imprisoned by Herod and awaiting death, struggles to understand a Lord who did not live up to his expectations.

If you are a suffering Christian or know of one, this book will bring enormous comfort and insight into the ways of God.

A Tale of Three Kings
Gene Edwards

Myriads of Christians have experienced pain, loss and heartache at the hands of other believers. This compelling story offers comfort, healing and hope for these wounded ones. Probably more Christians have turned to *A Tale of Three Kings* for healing than to any other book for decades.

This simple, powerful, and beautiful story has been recommended by Christians throughout the world.

Library of Spiritual Classics

Jeanne Guyon wrote *Experiencing the Depths of Jesus Christ* around 1685. For over three hundred years, this book has led untold numbers of Christians to the riches of fellowship with Jesus Christ.

This little book on prayer will revolutionize your relationship with the Lord.

We have received thousands of calls and letters from Christians impacted by the writings contained in this book. The most prevalent comment is, "I can experience and know my Lord today in a real way."

Union with God contains Jeanne Guyon's spiritual progression in the Lord. She reveals her desire to love only Jesus Christ, to live only for Him, and to suffer for Him. In her abandonment to her Lord, she acknowledges all things from the hand of her beloved.

Guyon reminds us that the Lord dwells within…and within is where we seek him…and there enjoy him in oneness.

You will marvel at Guyon's devotion to Jesus Christ, a devotion that she desired all believers to have towards the Lord.

We have included twenty-two of her poems that reveal a vast depth of love and understanding as to the ways of God. *Union with God* will point you to that place of infinite peace found only in Jesus Christ.

Fenelon lived during the period of Louis XIV in the 1600's. *The Seeking Heart* is an updated version of a series of spiritual letters Fenelon wrote to seekers of his time. Although written to individuals concerning a specific issue, the spiritual wisdom and counsel contained within these letters make them relevant for today. (The same is true concerning Paul's letters in the New Testament.)

After having read *The Seeking Heart*, you will come away moved by Fenelon's belief that God was in all things in his life. . . things fair and things unfair. He invites us to share this Christ-centered way of life.

Library of Spiritual Classics

The two best books in print in the English language on the *practical* aspects of the deeper Christian life are *Experiencing the Depths of Jesus Christ* and *The Spiritual Guide*. Both books appeared in the mid 1600's, yet neither author knew the other.

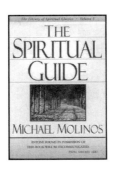

Molinos was tried and condemned and then sealed in a dungeon in Rome for writing this book. Afterwards, his books were burned. Nonetheless, *The Spiritual Guide* remains one of the great treasures of Christian history. Readers find this book to be transforming.

Next to *Experiencing the Depths of Jesus Christ*, this is the most *practical* book in print on the "how" of knowing Christ.

Be introduced to the joy of living constantly in the presence of the Lord.

Brother Lawrence experienced such joy while surrounded by kitchen pots and pans in the monastery to which he belonged. No job was too menial for him: "…to pick up a piece of straw was to do it unto the Lord."

First published in French in 1692, this little book has guided countless thirsty souls to a deeper and closer walk with God. SeedSowers publishes the easiest-to-read updated version of this timeless classic.

We have added excerpts of the letters of Frank Laubach's book, *Letters by a Modern Mystic*. Laubach lived as a missionary in the Philippines during the 1930's and practiced living in the Lord's presence.

 SeedSowers Publishing House

P.O. Box 3317

Jacksonville, FL 32206

1-800-228-2665

www.seedsowers.com

SEEDSOWERS
800-228-2665   (fax) 866-252-5504
www.seedsowers.com

REVOLUTIONARY BOOKS ON CHURCH LIFE

Beyond Radical *(Edwards)* 7.95
How to Meet In Homes *(Edwards)* 10.95
An Open Letter to House Church Leaders *(Edwards)* 5.00
When the Church Was Led Only by Laymen *(Edwards)* 5.00
Rethinking Elders *(Edwards)* 9.95
Revolution, The Story of the Early Church *(Edwards)* 11.95
The Silas Diary *(Edwards)* 9.99
The Titus Diary *(Edwards)* 8.99
The Timothy Diary *(Edwards)* 9.99
The Priscilla Diary *(Edwards)* 9.99
The Gaius Diary *(Edwards)* 10.99
Pagan Christianity *(Viola)* 13.95

AN INTRODUCTION TO THE DEEPER CHRISTIAN LIFE

Living by the Highest Life *(Edwards)* 10.99
The Secret to the Christian Life *(Edwards)* 9.99
The Inward Journey *(Edwards)* 10.99

CLASSICS ON THE DEEPER CHRISTIAN LIFE

Experiencing the Depths of Jesus Christ *(Guyon)* 9.95
Practicing His Presence *(Lawrence/Laubach)* 9.95
The Spiritual Guide *(Molinos)* 8.95
Union With God *(Guyon)* 8.95
The Seeking Heart *(Fenelon)* 9.95
Intimacy with Christ *(Guyon)* 10.95
Spiritual Torrents *(Guyon)* 10.95
The Ultimate Intention *(Fromke)* 10.00
One Hundred Days in the Secret Place *(Edwards)* 12.99

IN A CLASS BY ITSELF

The Divine Romance *(Edwards)* 11.99

NEW TESTAMENT

The Story of My Life as Told by Jesus Christ *(Four gospels blended)* 14.95
The Day I was Crucified as Told by Jesus the Christ 14.99
Acts in First Person *(Book of Acts)* 9.95

COMMENTARIES BY JEANNE GUYON

Genesis Commentary 10.95
Exodus Commentary 10.95
Leviticus - Numbers - Deuteronomy Commentaries 12.95
Judges Commentary 7.95
Job Commentary 10.95
Song of Songs *(Song of Solomon Commentary)* 9.95
Jeremiah Commentary 7.95
James - I John - Revelation Commentaries 12.95

THE CHRONICLES OF HEAVEN *(Edwards)*

THE COLLECTED WORKS OF T. AUSTIN-SPARKS

COMFORT AND HEALING

OTHER BOOKS ON CHURCH LIFE

CHRISTIAN LIVING